Edinburgh in colour

Introduction and commentaries by
JOHN
HUTCHINSON

featuring photographs by
Douglas Corrance

B.T.BATSFORD LTD
LONDON

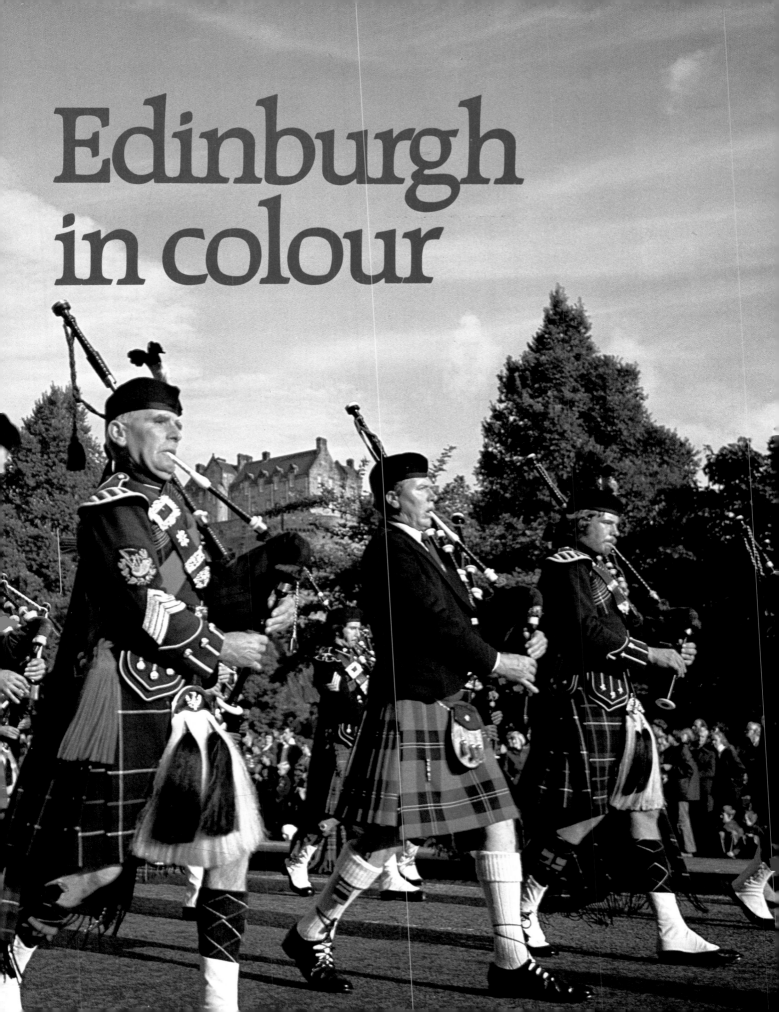

Edinburgh
in colour

First published 1980
© text John Hutchinson 1980
Filmset by Asco Trade Typesetting Ltd, Hong Kong
and printed by South China Printing Co., Hong Kong
for the Publishers B.T. Batsford Ltd,
4 Fitzhardinge Street, London, WIH OAH

ISBN 0 7134 1998 9

Frontispiece: Pipers in Princes Street

Contents

Acknowledgments

The Publishers are most grateful to Douglas Corrance in particular, to the Scottish Tourist Board, and to A.F. Kersting, for providing the colour transparencies from which the illustrations were reproduced

INTRODUCTION
-a city to live in

Generations of commentators on Edinburgh, from
Cockburn to Daiches, have written about the city and
described in great detail the attractions of living in it;
but it was Robert Louis Stevenson, in particular, who
captured the mellow quality of the people and of life
in Edinburgh: that timelessness which was so clearly
a part of Edinburgh life when he was writing his book
Edinburgh nearly a century ago, and is still a part of
Edinburgh life today. It is indeed remarkable how
little the city, its life and its people have changed over
that century.

There is, within most citizens of Edinburgh,
a strong sense of conservatism and permanence and
an unwillingness to see any unnecessary change, which
has been for generations the despair of planning
consultants and dreamers of urban motorways. They
prefer to patch up or restore and to blend the old with
the new, rather than force the one to sweep the other
away. The University houses departments with names

out of science fiction in quiet Georgian back lanes;
old, unneeded churches are turned into concert halls,
commercial premises and electricity sub-stations; new
commuter roads are made on long-neglected railway
lines. So the basic tenor of life can go on, apparently
unruffled by technological change.

Yet Edinburgh is in its own way a pioneering city.
Over the centuries it has led the world in the development of municipal institutions now taken for granted.
In 1824 it set up the world's first city fire brigade
under James Broadwood. In the 1860s it had one of
the earliest and most famous medical officers of health,
Sir Henry Littlejohn, and its water supply from
reservoirs in the Pentland Hills was years ahead of its
time. Education, as might be expected, was also
advanced. The Edinburgh School of Arts (1821) was
one of the earliest Mechanics Institutes and nursery
education was pioneered in the Canongate at the
beginning of this century. And never let it be forgotten
that the Edinburgh Society of Chartered Accountants,
begun in 1854, was sixteen years ahead of its English
rival.

Conservative yet pioneering: this is just one of the
many contrasts in the city's complex character. There
is throughout a series of balances and counterbalances
fascinating to the observer and immensely enriching
to the life of its people.

It is, as Stevenson noted, parochial yet international: 'half a capital and half a country town'. Few capital cities have farms and beaches only five miles from their centres; few have sheep grazing on a city park and a major wild bird sanctuary in their midst. But as a major world legal, financial and cultural centre, its outlook is at the same time international, its institutions multi-lingual, its airport busy. *The Scotsman*, published in the city, reflects this, managing to include in its pages both reports from foreign correspondents on all matters of international concern and arguments in the letters column more suited to a village weekly.

Like most cities, it has engulfed once autonomous villages in its development; but, fortunately for the city, many of these villages remain as identifiable places, and not just as names on a map of suburban sprawl. Cramond, with its black and white buildings, sits out on the Firth of Forth, a haven for yachtsmen and summer-evening drinkers; Corstorphine jealously guards its fine medieval church; Dean, with its ancient mills, is an oasis five minutes' walk from Princes Street; Swanston, to everyone's surprise, has thatched cottages.

Italians call Edinburgh a sad city. Popular legend has forever dubbed it Auld Reekie. The air is cleaner now, but the city's dark grey buildings on a dark grey November day do indeed draw forth melancholy thoughts in a montage of grey on grey – grey skies, grey streets, grey people; a gloomy picture made gloomier by that peculiar phenomenon – the Edinburgh Sunday, the greyest day of all.

Stevenson wrote at length of the deadening effect that Sunday had on the people of Edinburgh, and the effect is, alas, still with us. Restaurants close, the streets are empty, entertainment and bustle are banished. Only the lonely speakers up on their platforms at the foot of the Mound and the inevitable pigeons show that there's life in Princes Street. People hurry on, as if a bit ashamed to be out, and disappear round the corner.

But if there's Sunday, there's always Saturday; and if there are dull November days there are also May and June. Clear blue skies light up another city and the sun sparkles on the stonework and through the leaves, as the bracing air of early summer brings out the cotton skirts and sandals. Surely, if climate has anything to do with the vigour and energy of a people, such days must be highly productive in Edinburgh.

Summer brings forth its ever-increasing array of visitors, each adding a touch of friendliness and novelty to the city, as they fill its streets. Some residents complain, as some always will, but fortunately there is no lack of space, and the visitors' is a positive contribution to the city's year. They offer colour and humanity to enliven its sober facade; they force its citizens out of their shells, and prepare them for the greatest deluge of them all, the Festival.

Heriot Row: Stevenson's House

Who can describe the diversity of the Festival, that annual blitzkrieg of culture? And who can explain how so extraordinarily vigorous a phenomenon has developed in what so many say is such an un-vigorous city? The Festival without doubt is one of Edinburgh's greatest contradictions and one of its greatest assets, bringing thousands of people to the city and influencing for the rest of the year both its cultural life and its finances. Play upon play, ballet, opera, music, revues, exhibitions, films, the Tattoo and an enormous miscellany of other events jostle together in a three-week marathon of things to see and do morning, noon and night. Few have the stamina, never mind the money, to see a quarter of what is offered, and few can honestly say that there was not something which interested, amused or stimulated them.

Such contrasts and contradictions lead inevitably to divisions: few people are ambivalent in their attitude to the city. There are those who love its ordered elegance, both architectural and social, and who enjoy the kind of inbreeding which makes it a poor day indeed if, on a walk down Princes Street, they don't meet someone they know. Some prefer its lack of commercially-provided nightlife and naturally turn themselves inwards to entertain at home. Some love the predictability of the city and its society and feel a sense of security there; others find it a stifling

Cramond

monument to middle-class snobbery, a *dreich* society in a *dreich* city.

But what of living in one of those solid stone-built late Victorian terraces? Tenements they're known as, without any of the slum connotations of elsewhere, tenements with common stairs and landings leading to hundreds and hundreds of purpose-built flats: not flats of the English variety, like glorified bed-sits, but grand and spacious with high ceilings, fine plaster-work, large drawing rooms and so often uniformly tiny bathrooms.

Brass name-plates, polished smooth over the years, appear in rows above the bell-pulls at the foot of the stairs or on the front door itself, proudly bearing the name of the occupiers, far more useful than a mere anonymous number. Heave at the heavyweight bell-pull and you set in motion a complex chain of wires, pulleys and levers worthy of Heath Robinson and which culminates in a brass bell dangling on a coiled spring right up in the kitchen. Another lever, this time on the landing and operated from inside, opens the outer door for you: a system to do credit to the Victorian engineer.

Cleanliness and hygiene were clearly in the minds of those now forgotten men who generations ago set the pattern for so much of tenement life in Edinburgh. Few kitchens are without a pulley, large enough to take a family wash when it's raining outside. The

The Edinburgh Military Tattoo at the Castle

draughty casement windows also swing inwards on
ingenious hinges to make them easier to clean,
a process which would otherwise require some courage
four floors up. The stairs too require to be cleaned,
a process which is regulated by the mysterious ritual
of the little card hung on your door knob announcing
'It is your turn to clean the common stair'.

Shared drying greens at the back, often of considerable size, also demand their own processes of
regulation, at times like a medieval village moot,
as decisions are made about cutting the grass, pruning
the trees, mending walls and fences and, more
recently, planting and harvesting vegetables. Each
stage needs to be planned and consulted and discussed
before action is taken. But not all things can be
regulated on a smooth year-to-year basis. Who tells
the lady in number seventeen to take her washing line
in at night? Who gets the mower mended and who on
earth trampled on my young broccoli last night?

Living in a top flat, in particular, brings its own
way of life, this time largely regulated by the sixty or
so stone steps to be climbed to your front door.
Traditionally, young couples start their married life
in a top flat and work downwards as their prosperity
increases and their vitality declines. Certainly, when
you live in a top flat can be sure that if your friends
bother to come and see you, they are good friends
indeed.

Princes Street Gardens: the Scott Monument

Life at the top has other advantages. Burglars would need to be air-borne to penetrate the windows and few strangers can climb the stairs without someone noticing. The doors open just a fraction, or a curtain is pushed back – eerie yet comforting in a way.

Ask the reason why someone enjoys living in Edinburgh and time and again the answer will contain the phrase 'quality of life'. There is the opportunity in Edinburgh to follow a life style in an environment which in other cities would only be available at twice the cost. The Georgian and Victorian squares and terraces of the New Town and beyond, and the 'medieval' lands of the Old Town offer the kind of housing to thousands which is available only to the few elsewhere. The privilege of living close enough to walk to work, or to a main shopping area like Princes Street, and yet of having large elegant rooms and a garden, is rare and usually very expensive in other cities. In Edinburgh that quality of housing, should you wish it, is available and unlikely to be destroyed.

Fortunately for all, so much of that elusive 'quality of life' is free. The city centre is rich in parks and gardens offering green foliage to soften the regular grey buildings and breathing space for residents and commuters alike. Lunchtime in Princes Street Gardens on a June day brings out thousands of office workers to soak up the sun and admire the view, the dramatic

The Cafe Royal

The Growth of the City

The City of Edinburgh grew eastwards from the Castle, down the long slope which is now the Royal Mile. By the mid-1400s it had spread halfway down, with the entirely separate burgh of the Canongate extending up the hill from the Palace of Holyroodhouse at the bottom. The two met at the Netherbow Gate which stood near the St. Mary's Street of today. The name of the last close before the gate, 'World's End Close', signifies what the burghers of Edinburgh thought of their neighbours in the Canongate.

Robert the Bruce gave the city its present charter as a Royal Burgh in 1329, though an organised form of burgh life had existed long before that; and the city became firmly established as the capital of Scotland around 1450 after successive kings had taken their Courts to Scone, Stirling, Perth and elsewhere.

Pressure was further increased by the need to build within the city walls, the last of which, the Flodden Wall, had been hurriedly constructed at the

time of the great Scottish defeat by the English at
Flodden Field in 1513. Houses became tenements and
tenements grew ten or twelve storeys high. Narrow
streets, closes and wynds let in less and less light as
sanitation, water supplies and street cleaning
increasingly failed to cope with the refuse. The city
acquired an evil reputation.

By 1750, there were 50,000 inhabitants, but the
tide began to turn. Greater affluence and a greater
desire to escape the smells of the Royal Mile
encouraged speculative building in the new, spacious,
Georgian style. George Square was built, then the
glorious and carefully planned development of the New
Town, with its gracious squares, crescents and circuses,
its tree-lined streets, parks and elegant way of life.
Gone was the social proximity of the Royal Mile with
all classes living close together. Instead Edinburgh
developed desirable areas and less desirable ones, a
feature which was further developed in the Victorian
era and which, though fashions in housing change, is
largely still with us today.

THE OLD TOWN

The Castle

It is customary and sensible to begin the description of the city where it all began, at the Castle.

The Castle on its hill is at the centre of all things in Edinburgh, if only because you have always to go round it to cross the city. But more than that, it dominates the city and its life as much today as it has done for a thousand and more years. It stands boldly on the city's coat of arms; its gun booms out at one o'clock; and directions are given using it as a marker.

The present building stands over 400 feet above sea level on the basalt rock of a volcanic plug. To the east, the gentle slope of the Royal Mile forms, with the Castle Rock, the classic example of a 'crag and tail', created as glaciers swept eastwards down what is now Princes Street Gardens and the Cowgate. The Picts are thought to have fortified the site around 400 AD, calling it Dun Edin, 'the fortress on the slope', but when the invading Angles coming from Northumbria took over the site in the seventh century, its name

29

changed to the more Germanic form, Edwinesburghe,
possibly after Edwin, their king. Of the Pictish and
Anglian fortresses, nothing remains save the names.

The earliest building remaining on the site today is
St. Margaret's Chapel, a remarkable survivor of 900
years of turbulent history. It was built in 1076 by
Saint, Margaret, the Saxon queen of Malcolm III,
'Canmore', the son of Duncan, murdered by Macbeth.
The simple rectangular chapel in Romanesque style,
is still in use. Beside it stands the unmistakeable shape
of *Mons Meg*, a fifteenth-century cannon weighing
five tons, which is known to have fired a salute when
Mary, Queen of Scots became engaged to the Dauphin
of France. It burst when firing a salute in 1683 and
its remains were carried off to the Tower of London
in 1759. Amid great drama it was returned to
Edinburgh in 1829, largely due to the efforts of
Sir Walter Scott, and with full military honours
took its place in the castle, there to be climbed upon
by generations of visitors.

Guns still form a major part of the castle's daily
routine. At one o'clock precisely, or perhaps it should
be called 1300 hours, a gun is fired from the Half
Moon Battery to give the people of the city their daily
time-check. Look for the puff of smoke, followed by
the bang, as locals check their watches, pigeons fly up
and startled visitors look around. 21-gun royal salutes
provide a less regular though even more noisy

following page: The Castle from Princes Street

The Royal Mile

The street which runs from the Castle to the Abbey
and Palace is, in true Edinburgh style, given a variety
of names along its length. It is at times Castlehill,
Lawnmarket (where lawn and other fabrics were
sold), High Street, Canongate (named after the Canons
at Holyrood), with the Castle Esplanade and Abbey
Strand at opposing ends. But always it is known as the
Royal Mile. Few streets in the world convey so
powerfully an atmosphere of unchanging history. The
high grey-stone tenements still look down on the
street below as they have done for more than three
hundred years. On occasions of state procession,
medieval banners are unfurled, the cobbles are covered
with sand for grip and the horse-drawn carriages and
mounted escort form a tableau of vivid spectacle.

Robert Burns, David Hume, John Knox and so
many more of the great figures of Scottish history have
in their time lived in the street itself or in the maze of
narrow closes, wynds and lands running off at right

angles. Built originally around the gardens of the
mansions and merchants' houses, each of these alleys
is a fragment of the city's history, faithfully recorded on
a plaque at its entrance. Here, in the hundred or so
alleys, is medieval Edinburgh, and the only way to see
it is to walk.

A long, slow walk down the Royal Mile is also an
exercise in the infinite variety of styles of architecture
reflecting the changes in taste and domestic living
from the 1500s to today.

Clinging to the east end of the Castle Esplanade
and by the Witches' Fountain are *Ramsay Gardens*,
built largely in nineteenth-century vernacular style,
and named after Allan Ramsay, the eighteenth-
century Edinburgh poet who had built a strange
octagonal house for himself on the site, a house
nicknamed 'Goose Pie Lodge' by his contemporaries.

By it are the *Camera Obscura*, which offers a
fascinating view of the city, and *Mylne's Court*, a
seventeenth-century tenement, built by the family of
Royal Master Masons involved in many major
building works all over Scotland, including Inveraray
Castle and the Palace of Holyroodhouse. The Court
has recently been restored as housing for university
students and many original details like the half
window, half shutter, have been carefully replaced.

Across the road, *Riddle's Court* was the scene of an
early student riot, when in 1595 the boys of the Royal

West Bow

High School staged a sit-in, with tragic consequences. Next door is *Brodie's Close*, named after Deacon William Brodie, the prototype of Jekyll and Hyde, carpenter and town councillor by day, burglar by night. Brodie was hanged in 1788 on a gibbet he had designed himself. He is chiefly remembered today by the pub bearing his name, and what greater fame can a Scotsman have?

Lady Stair's House, built in 1622 and restored in the nineteenth century, now houses a museum of relics of Scott, Burns and Stevenson; and another facet of Edinburgh life is displayed to great effect in *Gladstone's Land*, a fine example of an Edinburgh merchant's house of the seventeenth century. Outside stairs, arched piazza, crow-stepped gables and painted ceilings were all common features of urban houses of the time, reflecting the strong links between eastern Lowland Scotland and the Low Countries. Today the building is restored and furnished in period style.

St. Giles is the High Kirk of Edinburgh, the city church. It was created a Cathedral under the brief ascendancy of the Episcopal Church in the seventeenth century, but although the charter has not been revoked, the title is incorrect. The Episcopal Cathedral in Edinburgh now is the three-spired St. Mary's in Palmerston Place. St. Giles has had many ups and downs in its life, having been at one time a court, shops, prison, police station and divided into three

Lady Stair's Close

separate churches. It has survived all that, and a
drastic restoration in the nineteenth century, and is
today dignified and respected, if a little sombre and
drab, with its crown spire standing high above the
surrounding buildings. One of its most notable parts is
one of the most recent, the chapel, built by Sir Robert
Lorimer in 1911, of the Most Ancient and Most
Noble Order of the Thistle, Scotland's highest order of
chivalry.

By its west door, in the paving stones, is traced out
the *Heart of Midlothian*, which marks the entrance to
the Old Tolbooth or prison originally built in 1466.
The Tolbooth was demolished in 1817 and the
gateway was incorporated by Sir Walter Scott into
his mansion, Abbotsford. The name survives in many
ways, notably as one of Edinburgh's major football
teams.

At the east end stands the *Mercat Cross*, the focal
point of the city in medieval times. This was the place
of execution and of dissemination of public
information, a function still observed today. Royal
Proclamations are still read by Lord Lyon, King of
Arms, standing with his Lyon Court on the platform
restored last century by the Prime Minister, W.E.
Gladstone.

Behind the Mercat Cross and St. Giles and
contrasting with their medieval architecture, are the
classical facades of *Parliament House*, the *Signet Library*

St Giles

and other buildings of the Scottish Law Courts. The Scots Parliament met in Parliament House from 1639 till the Act of Union in 1707. Now it houses part of Scotland's legal system, with its supreme courts, the Court of Session for civil matters and the High Court for criminal ones.

The independence of Scots Law, which is different from the English and based more closely on Roman Law, is guaranteed by the Act of Union and has been vigorously defended, together with the Church, over the centuries. Scots lawyers may style themselves W.S., Writer to the Signet, or S.S.C., Solicitor in the Supreme Courts. Sir Walter Scott was a lawyer in these courts and also Librarian in the Signet Library. Today lawyers still pace up and down the Parliament Hall under its magnificent hammerbeam roof much as they did in Scott's day, still watched over by the great lawyers of the past whose portraits line the walls, and occasional chamber concerts are heard within the elegant classical walls of the Signet Library.

Charles II, they say, parades in Roman splendour on horseback outside Parliament House. Considerable debate there may be about who the statue actually represents, but there is no doubt that the lead statue, erected by the Town Council in 1685, is particularly old and that its legs used to buckle. A statue of John Knox stands less flamboyantly in the corner.

St Giles: Thistle Chapel

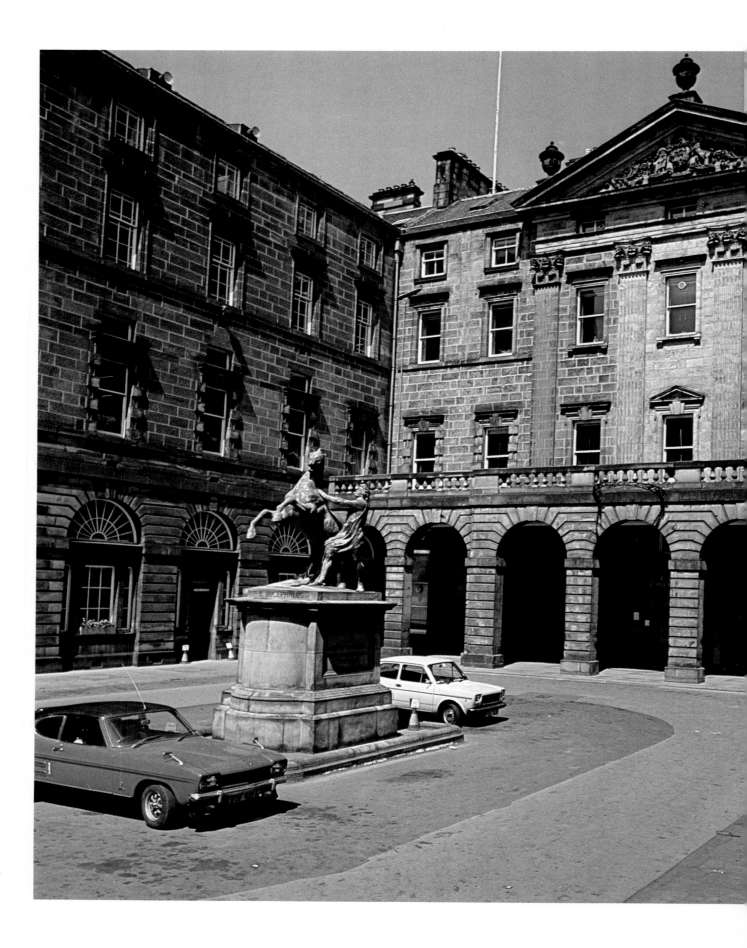

The elegant Palladian building across the road, which is now part of the *City Chambers*, was originally erected in 1753 as the Royal Exchange, and down its east side in *Anchor Close*, a printer called Smellie produced between 1768 and 1771 a compendium of knowledge which he called the Encyclopaedia Britannica.

The *Tron Church*, built in 1637, is a further reminder of the medieval commercial life of the city. It is named after the 'tron' or weighbeam which stood outside, where merchants had their weights checked and to which those erring were nailed by the ears. The original tower was destroyed by the fire which ravaged this part of Edinburgh in 1824.

John Knox's House, like the reformer himself, stands out clearly from all others, down the High Street beyond the Bridges. The house was built in 1490 and is in the typical style of the time, stone-built with overhanging, painted timber galleries, painted ceilings, an outside stair and an array of mottoes and a marriage plaque on the outside. Inside is a museum of relics of the reformer who, it is believed, occupied the house in the 1560s. Across the road, the *Museum of Childhood* is a welcome antidote to strict Calvinism and a real treat for parents, and their children as well. There, in an extraordinary jumble, is every childhood toy you can remember, and more, in an enormous collection of things relating to childhood through the

City Chambers

ages and through the world.

There are more museums further down what is by now the Canongate. *Huntly House*, a fine restored timber building of 1517, with religious mottoes on its walls, is the City Museum; next door is *Acheson House*, dating from 1633, now the Scottish Craft Centre, and nearby, *Moray House*, built in 1628 for the Dowager Countess of Home, was one of the last large private mansions in the Canongate. Its elaborate plaster ceilings have been preserved, though the house has been engulfed by the teachers' college of the same name. Across the road, the *Canongate Tolbooth*, a prison and courtroom which dates from about 1591, reminds us that the Canongate was a separate burgh till 1856, and next door to it, the *Canongate Kirk*, a notable pre-Reformation church of 1688, displays all the influence of the Low Countries in that period. Its graveyard contains many famous figures including the economist Adam Smith, 'Clarinda', friend of Burns, Robert Fergusson, the poet who influenced Burns, Lord Provost George Drummond who was so largely responsible for the development of the New Town, and perhaps even David Rizzio, Mary, Queen of Scots' ill-fated secretary.

At the very foot of the Canongate, opposite Abbey Strand and the gates of the Palace, is an attractive restored block of seventeenth-century houses, part of which is *White Horse Close*, originally the starting point

John Knox's House

Signs for the Museum of Childhood and the Huntly House Museum

of the coach for London, and named, it is said, after Queen Mary's white palfrey. It had strong Jacobite links in Charles Stuart's time, but today its red pantiles, outside staircases and projecting gables look peaceful, colourfully decorated with tubs of flowers.

The Palace of Holyroodhouse began as the guest house for the Abbey of the Holyrood (holy cross), which was founded by David I in 1128 and which is now in ruins. As Edinburgh developed in importance so the Court began to spend more and more time in the city, at first in the Castle, then in the more comfortable Abbey guest house. By the early sixteenth century, during the glorious reign of James IV, the monastic buildings were transformed into a palace. Mary, Queen of Scots passed six momentous years there, years which included her religious arguments with Knox, her marriage to Darnley and the murder of Rizzio. It is from this period that the palace draws much of its romantic attraction. With the removal of the Court to London in 1603 much of the glamour left the Palace, though it was considerably rebuilt by Sir William Bruce for Charles II from 1671. Mary's rooms were left largely intact. Charles Edward Stuart held a levee there in 1745 and the palace had a new if brief reign of glory. George IV held a levee in 1822 on his infamous visit to Scotland, and Edward VII when Prince of Wales used it as a residence during his studies at the University.

Canongate Tolbooth

IN 1688 KING JAMES VII
ORDAINED THAT THE MORTIFICATION
OF THOS. MOODIE, GRANTED IN 1649 TO
BUILD A CHURCH, SHOULD BE APPLIED
TO THE ERECTION OF THIS STRUCTURE

Today it is the official residence of Her Majesty the Queen when in Edinburgh, and the Lord High Commissioner, the Queen's representative, lives there during the General Assembly of the Church of Scotland. It is still also used for investitures, state dinners and garden parties.

The Royal Mile, however, is not the only remaining part of the old town of Edinburgh. The *Grassmarket* is an attractive, tree-lined square, formerly a place of execution. A cross at the east end marks the spot where over a hundred Covenanters died for their religious beliefs in the 1600s. Burns and Wordsworth lodged there in the White Hart Inn, and Burke and Hare, the nineteenth-century body snatchers lived just off it. Today it has a dual character with smart antique shops, boutiques and carefully restored buildings standing beside decayed tenements and hostels for down-and-outs, all completely overshadowed by the dramatic walls of the Castle, which towers over its west end.

In the Cowgate, running from its east end, is the *Magdalen Chapel*, the chaplaincy centre for the Heriot Watt University, and most notable for containing the only example in Scotland of pre-Reformation window glass surviving in its original position. Nearby in Candlemaker Row is *Candlemakers' Hall* and the much loved statue of *Greyfriars Bobby*, the terrier who faithfully watched over the grave of his master, John

Canongate Kirk   *following page : White Horse Close*

The Vennel

George Heriot's School

The Assembly Rooms

Quad or College, was built between 1789 and 1834 to designs by Robert Adam and W.H. Playfair, on the site of Kirk o'Field, where Darnley, Mary, Queen of Scots' second husband, was murdered in 1566.

In the Cowgate, one of its buildings, *St. Cecilia's Hall*, is a small, oval chamber with low domed roof, built about 1762 by the Musical Society of Edinburgh. Concerts were held here till the hall was overtaken in importance by the far larger present *Assembly* and *Music Halls* in George Street. St. Cecilia's languished till it was recently restored to something of its former splendour and uses.

Many of the University departments are housed in *George Square*, built in 1766 and one of the first of the Georgian squares to be laid out by speculative builders as the Old Town became too crowded and too inelegant for a section of Edinburgh society. Though severely altered, it remains today a quiet, academic backwater.

THE NEW TOWN

The move to George Square was the forerunner of the massive exodus to the newly planned and constructed New Town, particularly in the years from 1770 to 1830. The idea of constructing an entirely new area of Edinburgh away from the Royal Mile was not new. Plans had been mooted in the reign of Charles II, but the Act of Union, and then the upheavals and uncertainties of the two Jacobite risings, had caused them to be delayed. By the 1760s the country was sufficiently stable, city finances sufficiently strong and the overcrowding problem even more acute. With George Square as an example, and a powerful Lord Provost, George Drummond, to take a lead, a visionary scheme was begun to build a new Edinburgh to the north, across the waters of the Nor' Loch, now Princes Street Gardens. An Act of Parliament of 1767 gave the Town Council the powers to go ahead with a competition for a street plan, which was won by a 23-year-old architect, James Craig.

His plan followed the classical lines and proportions
predominant at the time and remains largely intact
today. It forms a gridiron of parallel streets with
squares and gardens, all named to symbolise Anglo-
Scottish unity and to glorify George III and the House
of Hanover. Thus George Street, the central axis, is
flanked by Thistle and Rose Streets, and they by
Queen and Princes Streets. Frederick (George's son)
and Hanover Streets cross it, and at its ends were to be
St. Andrew and St. George Squares. Charlotte,
George's wife thought otherwise.

Charlotte Square was designed in 1791 by Robert
Adam and its north side is considered to be one of
Europe's finest street fronts. Number 6, Bute House, is
the official residence of the Secretary of State for
Scotland and number 7, the *Georgian House*, has been
lovingly restored and furnished by the National Trust
for Scotland in the style of 1796 when it was built.
It is a haven of peace, quiet and elegance amid the
modern commercial bustle of today's city centre.

St. Andrew Square at the other end is technically one
of the wealthiest squares in the world as it houses the
headquarters of a large number of banks, insurance
companies and other financial institutions. In its centre
is a column with a statue of Henry Dundas, 1st
Viscount Melville, the most powerful political figure in
Scotland in the 1780s. South of St. Andrew Square,
at the east end of Princes Street is *Register House*, built

between 1774 and 1789, again to the designs of Robert
Adam. There are housed the historical and legal
records of Scotland, some dating back to the thirteenth
century. The bronze equestrian statue of the Duke of
Wellington which stands in front is by Sir John
Steell, and gives those who enjoy playing with words
the description 'The Iron Duke, in bronze, by Steell'.
An annex, *West Register House*, has been created
from the former church of St. George's in Charlotte
Square.

Princes Street is one of the most famous and
attractive of all city streets, largely because of its
gloriously open prospect on the south side over the
gardens to the Castle Rock. The gardens are largely
below street level so there is little traffic noise there,
and even though the main railway runs through them,
the trains are rarely seen or heard. The gardens were
originally private, created when the Nor' Loch was
drained, for residents' use. Now they are open to the
public to enjoy the entertainment, take refreshment,
admire the flowers and the statues of Scottish worthies,
rest weary shoppers' feet, or to look at the *Floral
Clock*, first made in 1903, and the oldest in the world.

The gardens are cut in two by the *Mound*, a
curving hill connecting Princes Street to the Royal
Mile. It was begun, so the story goes, in 1781 by
George Boyd, a Lawnmarket clothier, as a shortcut for
his New Town customers. The Town Council officially

7 Charlotte Square

*following page: View showing Princes Street, the Castle,
[the National] Gallery and the Scott Monument*

sanctioned 'Geordie Boyd's mud brig' and ordered that the soil excavated from the foundations of the New Town houses then under construction should be dumped there; and over two million cartloads were. At the foot of the Mound stand the classical buildings of the *Royal Academy of Scotland*, designed by Playfair in 1823 and now occupied by the Royal Scottish Academy of Painting, Sculpture and Architecture, founded in 1826, who still hold their annual summer exhibition there; and the *National Gallery of Scotland*, again by Playfair, opened in 1859, where the small but very important and satisfying national collection of art is displayed. Beside them, in the car park, is Edinburgh's equivalent to Hyde Park Corner, where on Sundays speakers harangue the odd passer-by.

The only other major buildings on the south side of Princes Street are, at the east, *Waverley Station* itself and the grimly imposing *North British Hotel* with its famous tower clock which regularly strikes panic into the hearts of would-be rail passengers heading for the station, by appearing always to be five minutes fast. Not far away is the black Gothic spire of the *Scott Monument* erected in 1844 again to the design of a competition winner, George Meikle Kemp. The statue of Scott and his dog Maida is by Sir John Steell. At the west end stand *St. John's Church*, built by William Burn in 1817, and *St. Cuthbert's*, an ancient foundation, rebuilt by Hippolyte Blanc in 1894.

The National Gallery of Scotland

following page: Looking towards Calton Hill and the former Royal High School from the Canongate Kirk

Towering above the gardens, as is perhaps fitting, is the *Assembly Hall* where each year the General Assembly of the ministers and elders of the Church of Scotland meets. Beside it is the domed headquarters of the *Bank of Scotland*, another important part of that very dramatic skyline which runs from the Castle to *Calton Hill*. Standing on its summit are several of the buildings which form part of Edinburgh's image as the 'Athens of the North': the Playfair and Dugald Stuart memorials, the Observatory, the Nelson Monument shaped like a telescope, and the Napoleonic War Memorial, begun in 1822 to be a copy of the Parthenon in Athens and never completed. One Grecian copy which was completed is the very satisfying *Royal High School* by Thomas Hamilton, completed in 1829, once destined to be the home of the Scottish Assembly. Near it is the equally classical *Burns Monument*.

Two of the most notable of Edinburgh's many museums and galleries, the *National Museum of Antiquities* and the *Scottish National Portrait Gallery*, are side by side in Queen Street, and built in a florid Victorian style which contrasts sharply with the Georgian simplicity around them. Victorian simplicity on the other hand is readily appreciated in the iron columns and arches of the *Royal Scottish Museum* in Chambers Street, near the University. All these museums are full, in some cases to overflowing, of

Moray Place

treasures from Scotland's past as well as major items of world interest.

To the north of the original New Town, down the dipping hills of Dundas and Howe Street, lie the further extensions which were begun in about 1820 and continued in a dramatic way for the next twenty years. In that time, the *Second New Town*, based on Great King Street with Northumberland and Cumberland Streets and Heriot and Fettes Rows, was developed, together with Drummond Place and Royal Circus; the massive circuses of Ainslie Place, Randolph Crescent and, above all, Moray Place were built on the former Moray Estate, and the quiet, more secluded areas away from the city centre, along the Water of Leith: Ann Street, St. Bernard's Crescent, Saxe-Coburg Place and Warriston Crescent.

By the 1850s the emphasis had shifted to the western end of the New Town, where the solidly impressive streets, now dominated by the three spires of Sir George Gilbert Scott's *St. Mary's Episcopal Cathedral* (1874), were developed. Housing fashions, too, were changing, from the long, straight city-centre rows of the first half of the century to the Victorian villas in a suburban setting and the long, high streets of tenements which dominated the last three decades. In that time Morningside, Newington, Marchmont, Merchiston, Joppa and Portobello grew up, often at considerable distance from the city centre, but made possible by the development of first horse then cable trams and, to a lesser extent, by suburban railways.

Around the City

By 1900 Edinburgh was no longer a city divided into Old Town and New. A third area of suburban development had been created, spreading rapidly and relentlessly around the other two and completely engulfing them.

The 1920s and 1930s saw the introduction of the motor bus which in particular opened up the suburbs along the road to South Queensferry, previously prevented from development because trams never crossed the Dean Bridge. The move to the suburbs continued through the 1950s and 1960s, notably with large municipal housing schemes to the south and west, but the 1970s have seen, in a very tentative way, a reversal of this tendency and the increasing emphasis on maintaining the tradition of city-centre living which has always remained strong in Edinburgh

Partly for this reason, though the suburban development in Edinburgh is obvious, it has never grown to the extent of other British cities with

similar populations. The city remains compact with only five or six miles in most directions from Princes Street to the first farms. In addition, the suburbs are dotted with a variety of features of historical and scenic interest and beauty, which prevent their slipping into anonymity.

Of prime importance for its scenic beauty is *Arthur's Seat*, the extinct volcano in the *Queen's Park* which is so large that it is both in the city centre and in the suburbs simultaneously. It stands over 800 feet high and is surrounded by three lochs, Duddingston, St. Margaret's and Dunsapie, all in the Royal Park of Holyrood. The park contains a ruined chapel, a holy well, a bird sanctuary, and supports a flock of sheep which, combined with the lochs and dramatic hill-slopes, give the place an air of Highland grandeur. The view over the city particularly from the Radical Road, built in 1820 under charitable subscription by unemployed weavers who were notorious radicals, emphasises the extraordinary evenness of roof height in wide areas of the city and the importance still to the sky-line of church spires.

One feature which is also noticeable when Edinburgh is viewed from on high is the number of extensive city parks on all sides. To the south are the *Meadows*, part of which was created when the Boroughmuir Loch was drained. Close by, *Bruntsfield Links* proudly claims to be the oldest golf course in the

world still in use, with justification it would seem as the golfing tradition there is even older than on *Leith Links* where Mary, Queen of Scots is said to have played. Further to the south the *Braid Hills*, the *Hermitage of Braid*, and *Blackford Hill* all thrust extensive green fingers into city housing development. On the latter is the *Royal Observatory*, founded by the Astronomical Institute in 1818 and moved from Calton Hill to its present site in 1896. The Professor of Astronomy in Edinburgh University also holds the title of Astronomer Royal in Scotland.

In the west, Corstorphine Hill joins with the *Scottish National Zoological Park* to provide an area of parkland with a multitude of other interests. The zoo is one of Europe's largest and one of the city's major attractions. It is world-famous for its penguins, the largest breeding colony of Antarctic penguins in captivity, and has a well-loved Children's Farm, a new Lion House and enough to keep both parent and child absorbed for days.

North of the New Town, *Inverleith Park* stretches across many football and cricket pitches to the gates of the *Royal Botanic Garden*, the world-famous institution which grew originally from the Physick Garden of the University and represents the ancient and strong links between medicine and botany through the use of herbal remedies. Today the garden is better known for its rhododendrons, and provides

Swanston

plant houses displaying specimens from all climates and terrains as well as attractive walks for Sunday strollers coming from church, looking for a quiet corner to read their paper, or showing off their babies.

Add to this list the 20 or so golf courses, all within the city boundary and it is easy to see why the city has an air of greenery about it. Indeed there are far more trees than people.

There are other castles too: *Craigmillar*, begun in 1374 and much added to, is a fine medieval fortress which served as a summer retreat for Mary, Queen of Scots. The views from its battlements are impressive, and its many safe stone staircases are excellent for exhausting children. *Lauriston* is a castle of a different kind, more an attractive country house which has been added to a tower house, originally built about 1590 for Sir Archibald Napier. It stands in wooded grounds, particularly noted for spring flowers, overlooking the Forth.

But the feature which makes Edinburgh's suburbs most outstanding is the ring of little villages, each one with its own characteristics, which have maintained their own identity in the face of the encroaching city. Most cities are divided into areas or sections which roughly coincide with the ancient settlements which were formerly there; few have managed to keep them so complete.

Cramond is on the shores of the Forth at the

Dean Village

northwest of the city. It is a tiny white-washed village, huddled in a valley at the mouth of the River Almond, which manages to cram 2000 years of history into a very small space. The name comes from Caer-Almond, 'the fort on the Almond', which was a Roman station built about 142 AD, the foundations of which are still to be seen; the Kirk is medieval, as is the stark tower house; many of the houses are eighteenth-century industrial dwellings built for the workers in the iron mills which harnessed the power of the river; and the village boasts an excellent old inn. Today the area is a major sailing and recreation area with a tiny rowing ferry across to walks in the Dalmeny Estate.

On the other side of the city, *Swanston* is an extraordinary and unexpected collection of white-washed thatched cottages, clustered around a tiny village green in the foothills of the Pentlands. Here Robert Louis Stevenson spent his summer holidays. *Duddingston* maintains an air of rural isolation despite being only a few minutes drive from the heart of the city. Set on the loch at the edge of the Queen's Park, the village has a twelfth-century church with ancient houses and inn. Outside the kirkyard there are jougs (an iron collar and chain used to punish malefactors), a watch tower (to protect the graves from body-snatches) and a loupin-on stane (to help elderly horsemen mount). Even closer to the centre, indeed almost underneath it, is the *Dean Village*, the old grain-milling centre for Edinburgh.

Only five minutes' walk from Princes Street and under the arches of Telford's impressive Dean Bridge (1832), the much restored and attractive village is one end of a lovely walk along the Water of Leith to St. Bernard's Well, a chalybeate mineral well erected in 1789 by Alexander Nasmyth.

Corstorphine, with its attractive High Street and medieval church; *Newhaven*, with its characteristic fishermen's cottages; and, further out, *Currie*, *Balerno* and *South Queensferry* are all distinctive in their characters, as are those important two areas on the coast, *Leith* and *Portobello*, once fiercely independent but now part of Edinburgh. Leith has for centuries been the main port for the city and the docks remain busy today. The street names resound with a nautical flavour: Baltic, Dock and Sandport Streets and The Shore itself, while the eighteenth-century Custom House, Trinity House and Exchange Buildings reflect the town's commercial importance, as does Lamb's House, a restored sixteenth-century merchant's house. *Portobello*, however, grew largely as a pleasure resort, then developed as an attractive residential suburb. 'Guid Auld Portie' was a traditional late nineteenth-century family holiday centre, and the birthplace in 1870 of Sir Harry Lauder. Today its broad sandy beach, parks, promenade and large swimming pool are still popular summer attractions; and again, remarkably close to the heart of the city.

Sport, Entertainment and the Festival

The outdoor facilities to be found at Portobello are
a strong reminder that despite its reputation as a
'cultural' city, Edinburgh is extremely sports-conscious
and particularly well endowed with sporting facilities,
many as a legacy of the highly acclaimed Commonwealth Games of 1970. The *Royal Commonwealth
Pool* and *Meadowbank Sports Centre* were both built
for that occasion and are now mainstays of the
city's sporting life. More surprising perhaps is the
largest dry ski slope in Europe which snakes down the
slopes of the Pentland Hills at *Hillend*. The chairlift
also offers wonderful views to non-skiers and is a
useful starting point for walks on the Pentlands.
Rugby enthusiasts make their twice annual pilgrimage
to *Murrayfield* to join with the exuberant Welsh and
French supporters or the more restrained English
and Irish in the international programme, while
soccer supporters don their green to watch Hibernian
(Hibs) or maroon to watch Heart of Midlothian

(Hearts) or even Meadowbank Thistle, Edinburgh's third league club. There is greyhound racing, speedway, golf, horse racing, motor racing, yachting, sea angling and even river fishing in the Water of Leith!

But it is as a theatrical, arts and musical centre that Edinburgh is perhaps best known, as the Festival legacy lives on through at least some of the year in the city's theatres, exhibitions and concerts. Major concerts are held in the *Usher Hall*, a solid elegant building where the Scottish National Orchestra gives its major programme of winter concerts and a summer season of proms. The *Royal Lyceum* is a turn-of-the-century theatre recently extensively refurbished in opulent style, which has its own resident company and a smaller theatre next door. The *King's* is another nineteenth-century touring theatre large enough to hold some major operatic performances. Smaller theatres include the *Traverse*, a private theatre club which has often been in the headlines for its performances, and *Calton Studios*, a modern auditorium suitable for a wide range of entertainments and functions. *Leith Theatre* and *Church Hill Theatre* also offer frequent theatrical and musical performances, often by amateur groups.

The long saga of the Opera House and the question of refurbishing the magnificent *Playhouse* go on. There is little doubt that, despite the numbers of theatres and halls available, there is a demand for more and this demand is never greater than during the three weeks of that extraordinary phenomenon, the Festival.

The Festival is the loose term given to what is really four festivals in one. The *Edinburgh International Festival* began in 1947 as a bold attempt to encourage reconciliation and to lift the depression following the Second World War. Since then it has grown into one of the world's major cultural events with performances of the highest international standards, in theatre, opera, music and ballet, and major international exhibitions.

The *Edinburgh Military Tattoo* is an evening performance of military and civilian groups on the Castle Esplanade with the glorious backcloth of the floodlit castle. Temporary grandstands are erected each year to enable thousands to witness the unforgettable sight of the massed pipes and drums and the emotion of the lone piper on the battlements. The *Edinburgh Festival Fringe* is a loosely organised collection of anyone who wishes to come to Edinburgh during the period around the International Festival to perform anything and everything. The Fringe has witnessed a tremendous growth so that over the three-week period hundreds of different companies and performers are offering many more hundreds of different plays, shows, happenings, reviews, exhibitions, with music, dance and many world and

British premieres – some never to be repeated. The *Edinburgh Film Festival* has also developed at a tremendous rate in recent years so that it too is one of the world's major events of its kind. Many international directors, producers and actors attend to discuss their work and 'seasons' concentrating on one particular theme or aspect of the cinema are offered.

The enormous growth and success of the Festival has firmly established Edinburgh as a modern centre of culture of world renown. Today it is also one of Britain's major tourist attractions, and these two complement its more traditional importance as an educational and architectural centre of excellence. The Athens of the North has not lost the virtues and talents which first brought it fame, but rather, in true Edinburgh style, has kept these ancient links, adapted them to modern needs, and, selectively and with care, added to them.

Following page: Edinburgh from Calton Hill at night

Index